How to Launch Your Own Successful eCommerce Store

A Step-by-Step Guide

Table of Contents

1. Introduction 1

2. Understanding eCommerce: A Primer 2

    2.1. The Basics: What is eCommerce? 2

    2.2. Why Go Online: The Benefits of eCommerce 2

    2.3. Developing Your eCommerce Business Model 3

    2.4. Laying Out your eCommerce Sales Strategy 4

    2.5. Building an Effective Marketing Strategy 4

    2.6. Understanding the Legal Aspects 5

3. Identifying Your Niche: Positioning Your Store for Success 6

    3.1. Why is Niche Identification So Important? 6

    3.2. Identifying Potential Niches: Where to Begin 7

    3.3. Understanding the Competition 7

    3.4. Evaluating Market Demand 8

    3.5. Validating Your Niche 8

    3.6. Final Thoughts 8

4. Creating Your Business Model: Plan for Profitability 10

    4.1. Understanding What a Business Model Is 10

    4.2. Building Blocks of an eCommerce Business Model 10

    4.3. Choosing the Right Business Model for Your eCommerce Store 11

    4.4. Crafting a Comprehensive Profit Model 12

5. Building Your Brand: Crafting a Powerful Identity 14

    5.1. What's In a Brand Identity? 14

    5.2. Building Your Brand Voice 15

    5.3. Crafting Your Visual Identity 15

    5.4. Determining Your Brand Personality 16

    5.5. Aligning with Brand Values 16

6. Choosing The Right eCommerce Platform: A Comparative

Analysis 17

6.1. Understanding Your eCommerce Business Needs ... 17

6.2. Cost vs. Value 17

6.3. Evaluating Platform Features 18

6.4. Analyzing Popular eCommerce Platforms 18

6.4.1. Shopify 18

6.4.2. WooCommerce 18

6.4.3. BigCommerce 19

6.4.4. Magento 19

6.5. Security and User Experience 19

6.6. Platform Scalability 19

7. Designing Your Online Store: User Experience for Success 21

7.1. Understanding User Experience 21

7.2. Research and Understand Your Users 21

7.3. Mapping the User Journey 22

7.4. Site Architecture and Navigation 22

7.5. Mobile First Design 23

7.6. Product Pages Design and Optimization 23

7.7. Shopping Cart and Checkout Process 24

7.8. Usability Testing 24

8. Product Sourcing and Inventory Management: The Logistics Conundrum 25

8.1. Identifying Suppliers and Building Relationships 25

8.2. Inventory Management 26

8.3. Choosing the Best Inventory Management Techniques 26

8.4. Implementing Technology in Inventory Management 27

8.5. Overcoming Inventory Challenges 28

9. Secure Payment Solutions and Shipping: Trust and Efficiency ... 29

9.1. Understanding Payment Solutions 29

9.2. SSL Certificate: A Must-have for All eCommerce Stores 30

9.3. Choosing the Right Shipping Solutions ... 31

9.4. Strengthening Trust with Efficient Returns Policy ... 31

10. Digital Marketing for eCommerce: Driving Traffic and Increasing Sales ... 33

10.1. Understanding Digital Marketing for eCommerce ... 33

10.2. Importance of SEO in eCommerce ... 33

10.3. Email Marketing Strategy ... 34

10.4. Utilizing Social Media Platforms ... 34

10.5. Influencer Marketing ... 35

11. PPC Advertising ... 36

12. Measuring Success with Analytics ... 37

13. Scaling Up: Managing Your Growing eCommerce Store ... 38

13.1. Set Clear Growth Goals ... 38

13.2. Develop a Scalable Business Model ... 38

13.3. Employ Automation ... 39

13.4. SEO Optimisation ... 39

13.5. Optimize Site Performance ... 40

13.6. Enhancing Customer Service ... 40

13.7. Adapting Business Plan ... 40

Chapter 1. Introduction

Introducing our comprehensive Special Report: "How to Launch Your Own Successful eCommerce Store: A Step-by-Step Guide". This in-depth guide is loaded with actionable insights and expert advice, specifically designed to help you turn your entrepreneurial vision into a successful online shopping destination. Whether you have an existing brick-and-mortar store or are starting from scratch, this report holds the keys to your digital kingdom. And don't worry; you need not be a tech wizard to get through it! Our step-by-step approach ensures that even the most technical concepts are broken down into digestible, easy-to-understand pieces. By purchasing this special report, you'll not only be investing in the transition of your business to an online powerhouse but also igniting a journey of growth, innovation, and untold possibilities. So, come aboard and let's turn your dream eCommerce store into a booming reality!

Chapter 2. Understanding eCommerce: A Primer

Online shopping has undergone an irrefutable metamorphosis in the last decade, swiftly segueing into one of the most profitable and dominant industries across the globe. Understanding the mechanisms that propel an eCommerce business is the foundational bedrock of creating a successful online store. Let's delve into it now.

2.1. The Basics: What is eCommerce?

eCommerce, or electronic commerce, can be succinctly delineated as the buying and selling of goods and services on the internet. Though the term was coined decades ago, its full scope has only been understood and exploited in recent years. eCommerce exists in various forms, including but not limited to:

- Business-to-Business (B2B)

- Business-to-Consumer (B2C)

- Consumer-to-Consumer (C2C)

- Consumer-to-Business (C2B)

Each type brings about its unique challenges and opportunities. Understanding which one aligns with your business is crucial to defining your target customers and the services you offer.

2.2. Why Go Online: The Benefits of eCommerce

In a world that's rapidly digitizing, it isn't just advantageous to have an online presence—it's necessary. With a brick-and-mortar store, your reach is largely localized. But with an eCommerce store:

- Your pool of potential customers transcends geographic bounds.

- You can be open 24/7, 365 days a year.

- It becomes easier to comprehensively track customer behavior and adapt accordingly.

- Minimized overhead costs mean maximized profits.

2.3. Developing Your eCommerce Business Model

Initiating an eCommerce venture isn't as simple as transferring your offline business online. It requires a thorough comprehension and careful crafting of your business model. A few pivotal elements include:

- Product or service: What are you selling? A physical product, a digital service, or both?

- Market study: What's the demand for your product? Who are your competitors? What's your USP?

- Pricing: How will you price your product or service? What's your cost of operation?

- Logistics: How will you store, package, and deliver your product? Or provide your service?

- Marketing Strategy: How will you reach and persuade your potential customers to buy your product or service?

2.4. Laying Out your eCommerce Sales Strategy

Your sales strategy is the blueprint that helps to convert your website's visitors into paying customers. A few elements to consider when putting together your sales strategy:

- Acknowledging customer pain points: Identify the problems that your product or service can solve.

- Potent product descriptions: Make sure they're informative and persuasive.

- Professional product images: These can significantly boost the perceived value of your product.

- Conversion-optimized website design: Your website should be as intuitive as possible.

- Customer reviews: Social proof massively increases trust and can significantly boost sales.

- Upselling and cross-selling: Strategically place related products to maximize your average order value.

2.5. Building an Effective Marketing Strategy

Attracting customers to your online business entails developing and implementing a potent marketing strategy. It hinges upon:

- Search Engine Optimization (SEO): Improving search engine rankings, thus garnering organic traffic.

- Pay-Per-Click (PPC) Advertising: Paid targeted advertising to drive potential customers to your store.

- Social Media Marketing (SMM): Harnessing the potent power of social media platforms to engage and draw in potential customers.

- Email Marketing: A direct line of communication with your customers, ensuring retention and conversion.

- Content Marketing: Providing valuable content can position your brand as an authority and eventually turn readers into customers.

2.6. Understanding the Legal Aspects

There are a few legal considerations you need to sieve through before launching your eCommerce store, comprising:

- Privacy Policies: Explaining how customer data is collected, used, and protected.

- Data Security: Implementing stringent measures to protect your customer's data.

- Intellectual Property: Protecting your business identity, products, and original content.

- FTC regulations: Evidencing claims made in advertising, and abiding by shipping and refund regulations.

By now, you should be equipped with a fundamental comprehension of what eCommerce is, and the core elements needed to propagate it. But remember, the pinnacle of successful businesses isn't achieved in a day. It's a series of trial and error, consistent optimization, and above all else, learning every day. As we delve into the nitty-gritty aspects in the upcoming parts of this guide, keep an open heart and mind. One step at a time, let's usher your business into the world of eCommerce.

Chapter 3. Identifying Your Niche: Positioning Your Store for Success

Establishing your eCommerce store starts with identifying your niche, a critical decision point that ensures your business finds its rightful place amid the vast digital marketplace's landscape. Tailoring your offerings to match the specific needs, preferences, and pain points of a particular group not only helps attract the right customers, but it also allows your store to stand out among your competitors.

3.1. Why is Niche Identification So Important?

Understanding your niche is critical because it gives your store a clear focus, making it easier for you to develop tailored marketing strategies to reach your target market. A well-defined niche allows you to develop products, services, and content that specifically address the interests, needs, and pain points of your target audience. Moreover, it facilitates the creation of a brand identity that resonates with your audience, fostering a sense of community around your store, leading to strong customer loyalty.

You can see the power of niches in some of the most successful eCommerce stores today. For instance, Etsy is a platform for handmade, vintage items and craft supplies, Zappos is famous for its staggeringly wide selection of shoes, while Warby Parker's focus is on affordable, stylish eyewear.

3.2. Identifying Potential Niches: Where to Begin

Identifying your niche isn't just about picking an industry or a product line. It's about digging deeper to discover a specific segment within a broader market that you can cater to. Here's how you can go about identifying your niche:

1. Brainstorm: Put down on paper all the industries, product categories, and services that interest you. Draw from your personal passions, professional experience, and areas of expertise.

2. Define Your Target Audience: Once you have a list of potential niches, identify the specific demographic or market segment that would be most interested in these industries, product categories, or services.

3. Identify Problems: Next, identify the problems or pain points that your target audience is facing within your chosen niches. You may have to do some market research to accurately identify these issues.

4. Evaluate Potential Solutions: Now, examine how well the existing products or services within your chosen niche address these problems. Look for gaps where your offerings could provide a better solution.

3.3. Understanding the Competition

An integral part of identifying your niche is understanding your competition. This involves knowing both direct competitors (those selling similar products or services to your target market) and indirect competitors (those offering alternative solutions to the same problems your target market faces).

Conduct a thorough competitor analysis, looking at their product range, prices, marketing strategies, customer service, and the overall user experience they offer. Try to identify areas where you can differentiate your eCommerce store and offer better value to the customers.

3.4. Evaluating Market Demand

Having a great idea for a niche is one part of the equation. The other part is ensuring there's a market for your products or services. Use Google Trends, Keyword Planner, and other market research tools to gauge the level of interest for your niche. Look at search volumes, trend data, and social media engagement levels to ascertain potential demand. Remember, too narrow a niche might not have enough potential customers, and too wide might be excessively competitive.

3.5. Validating Your Niche

Once you've identified a potential niche, validate it. This could involve setting up a landing page for your proposed product/service and gauging user interest through sign-ups or conducting customer interviews to gather feedback. You may also consider starting small, testing your product or service in local markets before scaling to a global audience.

3.6. Final Thoughts

Identifying a niche is just the first step in establishing your eCommerce store. It's an ongoing process that may need adjustments as your business evolves and as market conditions change. Keep an eye on trends, consumer behaviors, and competitors to ensure your niche continues to serve you well.

By carefully choosing your niche, you're not just deciding on what to sell. You're also determining who your customers will be, how you'll market to them, and how you can solve their problems. As such, give it the time and attention it deserves. With a well-chosen niche, you'll be well on your way to building a successful eCommerce store.

Chapter 4. Creating Your Business Model: Plan for Profitability

Every successful eCommerce store starts with a solid business model underpinned by a carefully crafted plan for profitability. When planning your online store, it's essential to step back and invest time in understanding the structure and dynamics of your business. By creating a profitable business model, you build a solid base on which the rest of your eCommerce store is built.

4.1. Understanding What a Business Model Is

A business model is a strategy that outlines how a business operates to make a profit. It consists of various elements, such as value proposition, customer segmentation, revenue streams, and cost structure.

To create your unique business model for your eCommerce store, you must integrate the different elements in a way that gives you a competitive edge. This strategy will establish the foundation of your online store, determining how you generate income and continue to stay profitable.

4.2. Building Blocks of an eCommerce Business Model

1. Value Proposition: This point addresses what your store will offer that is unique or superior to competitors. It tells customers why they should purchase from your store instead of others. Your

value proposition should outline the main benefit of purchasing from you, how you solve customer problems, and why you're a better choice than your competition.

2. Customer Segments: Identify and understand your target audience. By dividing your customers into segments based on common characteristics, you can tailor your marketing strategies and customize your offerings to fit their needs and preferences.

3. Channels: Determine how you'll reach your customers. Channels include a variety of touchpoints like your website, email marketing, social media, mobile applications, and more. Select channels that align with your target audience's preferences and behaviors.

4. Customer Relationships: These are the types of connections you'll establish and maintain with your customers. This may range from personal assistance to automated services. Excellent customer relations often lead to customer loyalty, which can translate into returning customers and a consistent revenue stream.

5. Revenue Streams: Pinpoint your income sources. This can be from the sale of physical or digital products, subscription fees, advertising income, or commission on third-party product sales.

6. Cost Structure: Understand the costs involved in operating your eCommerce store. These costs can be direct or indirect, and variable or fixed. A comprehensive understanding of your cost structure will ensure that your price point is both profitable and competitive.

4.3. Choosing the Right Business Model for Your eCommerce Store

Different types of eCommerce business models will suit different purposes, depending on various factors like your product, target customers, and market environment. Here are some common eCommerce business models:

1. B2C (Business-to-Consumer): Companies sell products or services directly to consumers. Examples include online clothing stores or online supermarkets.

2. B2B (Business-to-Business): Companies sell products or services to other businesses. This could take the form of a wholesaler platform selling to retailers.

3. C2C (Consumer-to-Consumer): Consumers sell goods or services to other consumers. Think online marketplaces or auction websites like eBay.

4. C2B (Consumer-to-Business): Consumers offer products or services to businesses. An example would be a freelancing platform where businesses contract individuals for services.

The business model you choose should align with your strategy, the nature of your products, and the type of customers you wish to serve.

4.4. Crafting a Comprehensive Profit Model

A profit model is an outline of how your eCommerce store plans to make a profit. It reveals the financial mechanics of your business. The primary components of the profit model are the revenue model and the cost structure.

To craft a comprehensive profit model:

1. Determine Your Revenue Model: Your revenue model identifies the ways your eCommerce store will make money. There are numerous revenue models to consider including sales, advertising, affiliate, subscription, or freemium.

2. Analyze Your Cost Structure: Figure out your cost structure by

highlighting the main areas where you will incur expenses. Understanding your costs will help you make better pricing decisions, ensuring that you sell your products at a profit.

3. Profit Margins: Once you know your revenue streams and costs, calculate your profit margins. This will give you an understanding of your profitability per item sold.

Meticulously crafting your comprehensive profit model will allow you to see the bigger picture. From each product's profitability through to your overall store margins, taking the time to map this out will give you a vital insight into the feasibility of your eCommerce plans.

With a clearly defined business model in place, you're ready to move on to the next step: creating a competitive and goal-driven marketing strategy that drives traffic to your store. By understanding your business model and profitability plan, you've set the stage for your eCommerce store's success. Keep this as your guide as you inch closer to launching your store and make adjustments as necessary based on any changes in your business landscape.

Chapter 5. Building Your Brand: Crafting a Powerful Identity

The first step in creating a successful eCommerce venture is making a strong, impactful, and distinctive brand. Your brand is the face and voice of your enterprise; it encapsulates your mission, values, and unique selling proposition. In the crowded online environment, a well-crafted brand identity can be the difference between standing out and blending in.

5.1. What's In a Brand Identity?

A brand identity represents your business's personality. It goes beyond your company name, logo, or slogan; it comprises all elements that create a particular image in the minds of your customers. Key components of your brand identity include:

- Brand Voice: The tone and style in which you communicate with your audience.

- Brand Personality: The traits and characteristics that give your brand a distinct feel.

- Visual Identity: Logos, colors, fonts, and imagery that help convey your message visually.

- Brand Values: The beliefs and principles guiding your business.

To build a powerful brand identity, you must clearly define these components and ensure they resonate with your intended audience.

5.2. Building Your Brand Voice

Your brand voice is the verbal part of your brand presentation. It aids in forming a connection with your audience and gives life to your brand values.

To establish your brand voice:

1. Conduct extensive research on your target market and analyze their language and communication preferences.

2. Define your brand's personality and use this to reflect in your verbal communication.

3. Create a style guide that sets standards for all your written communication — from product descriptions to Tweets.

5.3. Crafting Your Visual Identity

Your visual identity is what first grabs attention. It is pivotal in making a memorable first impression and builds immediate recognition.

To craft a strong visual identity:

1. Design a unique and recognizable logo that resonates with your brand's personality.

2. Choose a color palette that aligns with your brand emotions and values.

3. Select typography carefully, ensuring it aligns with your brand voice.

4. Develop a visual style guide to maintain consistency across all platforms.

5.4. Determining Your Brand Personality

Your brand personality is a set of traits that personify your brand. It helps customers relate to your brand and fosters customer loyalty.

To define your brand personality:

1. Identify your target audience and what traits would appeal to them.

2. Examine your products/services. What personality traits do they suggest?

3. Keep it authentic and consistent across all platforms and interactions.

5.5. Aligning with Brand Values

Your brand values are the guiding principles of your business. They define your motivation and give a sense of purpose to your brand.

To define your brand values:

1. Determine the core principles that your brand stands for.

2. Ensure your brand values resonate with your audience's values.

3. Implement these values in every aspect of your business, from recruitment to marketing tactics.

Remember, a strong brand identity is not achieved overnight. It takes time, consistency, and effort. A robust brand identity will resonate with your audience, differentiate you from competitors, and create a loyal customer base. Take the time to build a powerful brand identity, and it will be the cornerstone of your eCommerce success.

Chapter 6. Choosing The Right eCommerce Platform: A Comparative Analysis

Your first step to launching a successful eCommerce business is making an informed choice about the platform that's going to fuel your online store. Let's dive deep into the process of identifying the right eCommerce platform to suit your needs, and provide a comparative analysis of popular platforms available in the market today.

6.1. Understanding Your eCommerce Business Needs

Consider your business's unique needs before you determine any platform to go with. If you are transitioning from a physical store to an online setup, you might want a platform that easily integrates with your current systems, like inventory and accounting software. Start from scratch? Then, simplicity might be your priority. Make sure to list down all your requirements- be it in terms of web design, customer relationship management, marketing tools, or technical support. Once you've figured out what you'll need, you can begin evaluating different platforms against those requirements.

6.2. Cost vs. Value

Cost is a critical factor to consider when choosing an eCommerce platform. While most platforms have a base fee, the cost of add-ons, customizations, and third-party integrations could substantially add up. Also, factor in the transaction fees charged by the platform based on your sales volume. While considering cost, evaluate the value offered by the platform. A more expensive platform might come with valuable features your business needs, weighing in favor of the cost.

6.3. Evaluating Platform Features

Identify what features are built into the platform, what needs to be added on, or what can be integrated with third-party services. Key features to evaluate include content management, product catalog and browsing, shopping cart and checkout processes, customer management, order management, and built-in marketing and SEO tools. Look for features that will make your store stand out, like the ability to create custom promotions, product reviews, and rich media display.

6.4. Analyzing Popular eCommerce Platforms

Let's now delve into the specifics of the most popular platforms currently ruling the market: Shopify, WooCommerce, BigCommerce, and Magento.

6.4.1. Shopify

Shopify is a one-stop solution that produces a comprehensive eCommerce store without needing to understand the technological intricacies. What stands out about Shopify is the extensive Shopify App Store, which simplifies customization by enabling add on features. On the downside, it has a steep pricing curve, especially when you need advanced features.

6.4.2. WooCommerce

WooCommerce isn't a standalone eCommerce platform, but a plugin that transforms your WordPress website into a fully functioning online store. Its primary advantage lies in its seamless integration with WordPress, making it an excellent option for those already utilizing WordPress as their CMS. However, you may end up paying for several plugins to achieve desired functionality.

6.4.3. BigCommerce

BigCommerce excels in providing built-in features and eliminating the need for extra plugins or apps. It includes superior SEO features, multiple sales channel integrations, and endless customization options. Nonetheless, it's not as user-friendly as others and could be expensive for higher volume businesses due to their sales threshold.

6.4.4. Magento

Magento is a robust, enterprise-grade open-source eCommerce solution. It offers extensive customization, flexibility, and scalability. However, Magento might not be the right choice for beginners due to its complex development and high maintenance costs.

6.5. Security and User Experience

Ensure the platform you choose prioritizes security. SSL certificate, PCI DSC compliance, two-factor authentication, and regular platform updates are some crucial elements to look for. User experience should also be top-notch, with a clean design, intuitive navigation, seamless checkout process, and superb mobile compatibility.

6.6. Platform Scalability

Think long-term and ensure your platform can grow with your business. Scalability refers to the ability of the platform to handle more customers, more sales, and more traffic while maintaining excellent site performance.

Choosing an eCommerce platform is a significant decision that impacts your business, so thorough research is a prerequisite. Use demo versions, free trials, and case studies to inform your decision. Remember, there's no one-size-fits-all solution, and the best platform for your business is one that fits your unique needs and budget.

Chapter 7. Designing Your Online Store: User Experience for Success

The journey to creating a successful eCommerce store starts with grasping the fact that user experience (UX) is non-negotiable. It is the foundation on which customers' digital interactions with your brand are built. This understanding will guide your design decisions and ensure that your online store is not just visually appealing, but functional, accessible, and user-friendly.

7.1. Understanding User Experience

For your eCommerce store to be successful, visitors need to find what they are searching for quickly and effortlessly. This is where the concept of User Experience (UX) comes into play. UX is about creating a product that provides meaningful and personally relevant experiences to users. This involves the design of both the processes of acquisition and integration of the product, including branding, design, usability, and functionality.

When applied to an eCommerce context, this implies creating a website design that is simple, intuitive, and easy to navigate, ensuring a seamless shopping experience for your customers. This could mean the difference between converting a visitor into a customer or losing them to your competitor.

7.2. Research and Understand Your Users

Before embarking on designing your eCommerce store, invest time and resources to understand your users. This involves conducting market research, creating user personas, and understanding their needs and preferences. These insights bequeath you with the ability to design a website that resonates with your target audience and meets their expectations.

Start with demographic data, but don't stop there. Dive into the specific behavior patterns, goals, motivations, and pain points of your users. Gather data from various sources such as surveys, interviews, and user testing to create comprehensive user personas to serve as a guide during the design process.

7.3. Mapping the User Journey

Having understood your users, the next step is to map out their journey. This represents the entire process that a user goes through when interacting with your eCommerce store. This could start from when a user lands on your site, to browsing for products, adding items to the cart, and finally checking out.

User journey maps help you to identify key customer touchpoints, understand the path that users take through your website, and uncover areas of friction or confusion that could be hindering conversions. They allow you to design from the user's perspective, ensuring you create a seamless and enjoyable shopping experience.

7.4. Site Architecture and Navigation

A vital part of UX design is ensuring that your website is structured in a way that makes navigation intuitive. Your website's architecture should reflect your users' journey, ensuring they can easily find what they're looking for without getting frustrated.

Your navigation menu acts as a roadmap to your website. It should be clear, easy to understand, and categorized logically. Each category and subcategory should naturally lead to products, enabling customers to find what they are looking for with minimal clicks. Remember, a visitor's journey through your site should be smooth and effortless.

7.5. Mobile First Design

In an era where more people are shopping on their mobile devices than on desktops, having a mobile-optimized eCommerce store is crucial. This is what we call mobile-first design. This approach ensures that your site is optimized for mobile devices first and then scaled up to larger screens.

The mobile-first design comes with numerous benefits. It improves site load times, it's favored by Google for ranking purposes, and it captures mobile users, which constitute a significant portion of online shoppers.

7.6. Product Pages Design and Optimization

Your product pages play a critical role in the conversion process. They are where you showcase your products, provide essential details, and convince visitors to make a purchase. Every element on this page counts, from product images, descriptions, prices, to customer reviews.

Ensure that your product photos are of high quality and give a comprehensive look at the product. Item descriptions should be compelling and provide all necessary information. Moreover, displaying customer reviews can help build trust and eliminate any doubts potential customers might have.

7.7. Shopping Cart and Checkout Process

The last steps of the customer journey – adding products to the shopping cart and checkout – are where most eCommerce stores lose their customers due to a process that is complicated and tedious. Your priorities here are simplicity and transparency.

Make sure that your visitors can view their chosen items easily, know shipping costs upfront, and move to the checkout process without any hindrance. At checkout, ask only for essential information to complete the purchase. The fewer the steps and the simpler the process, the higher the likelihood of conversion will be.

7.8. Usability Testing

After implementing your design, conduct usability testing. This involves seeing how real users interact with your online store and gaining insights into any issues that might hinder them from accomplishing their tasks effectively.

Doing effective usability testing will help identify any obstacles or confusing aspects of your online store before they impact your sales or brand reputation. Make necessary adjustments and keep refining your UX for optimal results.

In conclusion, designing a successful eCommerce store requires a dedication to crafting an exceptional user experience. This calls for understanding your user's needs, mapping out their journey, implementing intuitive navigation, designing product pages that sell, simplifying the checkout process, and ensuring your site is mobile-friendly. Lastly, never forget the importance of testing and refining your UX design – it's a process that never really ends but continues to evolve as business requirements and user expectations change.

Chapter 8. Product Sourcing and Inventory Management: The Logistics Conundrum

Selling online is not just about having an attractive website or excellent customer service. A robust and scalable product sourcing and inventory management system forms the backbone of an eCommerce business. A well-defined system can help you manage your online selling business smoothly and support its growth.

8.1. Identifying Suppliers and Building Relationships

One of the initial steps is identifying potential suppliers who can provide the products you need at a competitive price. However, it's equally essential for the supplier to be reliable. Factors such as their supply capacity, lead times, quality assurance, financial health, and business ethics are crucial.

Document their responses for future reference and comparison. It can be done using a simple table such as:

Supplier	Product	Price	Lead Time	Capacity	Quality Assurance	Financial Health	Business Ethics
Supplier 1	Product 1	Price 1	Lead Time 1	Capacity 1	Quality Assurance 1	Financial Health 1	Business Ethics 1

Suppli er 2	Produ ct 2	Price 2	Lead Time 2	Capaci ty 2	Qualit y Assur ance 2	Finan cial Healt h 2	Busin ess Ethics 2

Once you've identified potential suppliers, establish relationships with them. Building healthy business relationships will help you negotiate better prices, terms, and services.

8.2. Inventory Management

When it comes to eCommerce business, efficient inventory management is vital for success. It's not about stocking your inventory, but about balancing the costs of stocking and possible stock-outs.

```
Inventory = Stock-on-hand + On-order - Backorders
```

The 'Stock-on-hand' represents the current inventory level, 'On-order' stands for products ordered but not yet received, and 'Backorders' are customer orders that cannot be fulfilled.

Your inventory management system should minimize costs and prevent under and overstocking. It's always better to have a sufficient safety stock to compensate for uncertain demand or suppliers' delay.

8.3. Choosing the Best Inventory Management Techniques

Different inventory management techniques can help keep inventories in check. Some of them include:

- Just in Time (JIT): This method seeks to minimize the costs of holding inventory by receiving goods only as they are needed in the production process.

- Economic Order Quantity (EOQ): This model aims to determine the ideal order quantity a company should purchase to minimize total inventory costs.

- ABC Analysis: This inventory management technique classifies inventory into three categories (A, B, and C), with A being the most valuable items, B being moderately valuable, and C being the least valuable.

- Dropshipping: In this model, the store doesn't keep the products it sells in stock. When a store sells a product, it purchases the item from a third party and has it shipped directly to the customer.

Each of these techniques has its pros and cons, and businesses should choose the one(s) that best fit their unique needs.

8.4. Implementing Technology in Inventory Management

Technology has made inventory management easier with automated tools and software. They help in tracking stock levels and predicting future demand, thus minimizing errors that may come with manual management.

It is wise to invest in an inventory management system that can integrate with your other business systems like eCommerce platform, accounting, and customer service. This way, you can streamline your operations and enhance business performance.

8.5. Overcoming Inventory Challenges

Every business faces unique challenges in its product sourcing and inventory management practices. Sometimes, the problem could be overstocking resulting in tied-up capital, while other times, it could be chronic stockouts leading to lost sales.

The best way to overcome these challenges is to have better visibility into your supply chain, improve demand forecasting, and adapt to changes quickly. It might also help to diversify suppliers to mitigate potential risks.

Product sourcing and inventory management can be the difference between running an eCommerce business smoothly and stumbling along the journey. By establishing strong relationships with suppliers, implementing efficient inventory management systems, selecting appropriate inventory management techniques, leveraging technology, and overcoming inventory challenges, eCommerce retailers can create a steady base for their business's smooth operations and continual growth. With precision and clarity at each step, you can ensure a consistent product flow, making for happy customers and a prosperous business.

Chapter 9. Secure Payment Solutions and Shipping: Trust and Efficiency

Online businesses can only thrive if they offer secure and reliable payment solutions and shipping options. They're the backbones of all eCommerce operations, as they engender trust and enhance efficiency. As we delve into this chapter, we'll be looking at various best industry practices, strategic decisions, and selections of tools and services that can either make or break your eCommerce venture.

9.1. Understanding Payment Solutions

The payment gateway is the heart of every eCommerce setup. It's the online equivalent of the payment terminal at physical stores. Essentially, a payment gateway is a service that authorizes and processes transactions in online shopping. Apart from accepting payments, a good payment gateway also comes with fraud detection features.

So, how does a payment gateway work? Whenever a customer places an order from an online store, the payment gateway performs a series of tasks to finalize the transaction:

1. The customer selects the product and proceeds to checkout.

2. They enter their payment details into the secure online form.

3. The web browser encrypts the data to be sent between it and the seller's web server. SSL (Secure Socket Layer) encryption technology is deployed for added security.

4. The gateway sends the transaction information to the vendor's

acquiring bank.

5. The transaction data is then forwarded to the issuing bank (the customer's bank).

6. The bank sends a response back to the gateway (approved or denied), and this gets relayed back to the website/cardholder. This process takes a few seconds.

7. The payment gateway then processes the customer's credit card for the price of the item they bought.

Some of the most popular payment gateways include Stripe, PayPal, Authorize.Net, Adyen, and Square. When choosing a gateway, make sure it supports all the payment methods popular with your target audience. Secondly, pay attention to the fees charged by the service.

9.2. SSL Certificate: A Must-have for All eCommerce Stores

An SSL (Secure Sockets Layer) Certificate is a digital certificate that authenticates the identity of a website and encrypts information sent to the server using SSL technology. The certificate serves two primary functions:

1. It authenticates the identity of the website, assuring your customers that they are not on a fraudulent site.

2. It encrypts the data that's being transmitted, including credit cards numbers, names, and addresses.

Therefore, having an SSL Certificate assures your customers that their sensitive information remains secure during transactions, thereby building their trust in your eCommerce site.

9.3. Choosing the Right Shipping Solutions

Just as important as taking payments, the delivery of your product also has a significant impact on customer satisfaction and your profit margins. When selecting a shipping solution for your eCommerce, you must consider the following:

1. Shipping speed: In the age of Amazon Prime's two-day shipping, consumers have high expectations about delivery times. While it may be challenging to match Amazon's speed, evaluate your supply chain to see where you can cut time without increasing costs.

2. Shipment tracking: Customers like to know where their orders are. Consider shipping solutions that offer tracking abilities to keep your customers informed about their packages' whereabouts.

3. Shipping costs: Consumers are always hunting for stores that offer free shipping. If your profit margins allow it, you should certainly consider this.

Remember, shipping doesn't end once the product leaves your warehouse. Customer service plays a crucial role in managing shipping inquiries and damage claims.

9.4. Strengthening Trust with Efficient Returns Policy

Just as important as the product is the after-sales service. A transparent, efficient, and fair return policy adds to consumer trust and helps build a lasting relationship with the customers. When designing your return policy, follow these guidelines:

1. Be Clear and Comprehensive: Explain clearly what items can be returned, under what circumstances, and within what timeframe.

2. Be Fair: Remember, an unfair return policy can backfire, leading to upset customers and damaging your brand image.

3. Display Your Policy Prominently: Don't hide your return policy in small print at the bottom of your website. Make it visible to all customers.

In conclusion, establishing secure payment solutions and efficient shipping options is integral for the success of your eCommerce business. By ensuring secure transactions, fast and reliable delivery, and fair return policies, you can build the trust of customers and enhance the efficiency of your business operations.

Chapter 10. Digital Marketing for eCommerce: Driving Traffic and Increasing Sales

The digital world is a bustling marketplace, teeming with opportunities for businesses that understand how to catch the eyes of potential customers. For an eCommerce store, understanding digital marketing—building a powerful online presence, mastering search engine optimization (SEO), leveraging email marketing, social media platforms and more—is critical in gaining this visibility, increasing website traffic, and driving sales.

10.1. Understanding Digital Marketing for eCommerce

Digital marketing involves using digital channels, devices, and platforms—no matter if they're online or offline—to build or promote your marketing message. In a broader sense, it also includes anything that involves digital communication.

An important aspect of digital marketing in eCommerce is understanding your customer life cycle, which involves awareness, consideration, purchase, retention, and advocacy. Each part of the cycle requires a different approach to marketing, but they all work together to boost your overall strategy.

10.2. Importance of SEO in eCommerce

Search engine optimization or SEO is about making your eCommerce store visible in the sea of competitors on search engines. When a potential customer uses a search engine like Google to find a product, SEO will determine if your shop appears on the first page of results. Essentially, SEO increases your online visibility and leads more traffic to your website.

Content is king in SEO but understanding search algorithms, using the right keywords, creating backlinks, and ensuring your website's loading speed and mobile optimization are high, also play crucial roles in your website ranking. Make sure to continually update your SEO practices as search engines often update their algorithms.

10.3. Email Marketing Strategy

Email marketing is not a thing of the past. In fact, it's one of the most effective marketing strategies for eCommerce businesses. It allows for targeted and personalized communication with your customers, resulting in higher conversion rates.

The first step to a successful email marketing strategy is to build an email list. You can do this by offering website visitors valuable content in exchange for their email address.

Once you have contacts to work with, create personalized emails to engage them. Your emails should not just be about selling your products, but offer value to the reader. Remember, the goal is to build trust and loyalty, which in turn creates repeat customers.

10.4. Utilizing Social Media Platforms

Social media platforms like Facebook, Instagram, Twitter and LinkedIn are tools every eCommerce business should be utilizing. With billions of active users daily, these platforms provide a massive audience for your products.

Social media advertising allows you to target your audience with precise criteria like location, age, interests, and more. You can also engage with your customers directly, reply to their queries or complaints, and foster a community around your brand.

Don't forget about the visual content! Utilize Instagram and Facebook stories or live video to showcase your products in a more interactive way.

10.5. Influencer Marketing

Influencer marketing involves partnering with influential people in your industry to expose your brand to their followers. These influencers can range from well-known celebrities to micro-influencers with a few thousand dedicated followers.

The credibility and relatability these influencers have with their audience can drive significant traffic and sales to your eCommerce store if done correctly. Be sure to choose an influencer who aligns with your brand's image and values.

Chapter 11. PPC Advertising

Pay-per-click advertising is another useful tool in your digital marketing toolkit. Platforms like Google Ads allow you to place your ads on search results, websites, or even product listings. You pay for these ads only when someone clicks on them.

For eCommerce stores, Google Shopping Ads are especially useful as they appear in direct response to someone searching for a particular product. These ads can include photos, prices, and a brief description of the product - all of which entice the user to click and buy.

Chapter 12. Measuring Success with Analytics

Lastly, but most importantly, is the role of analytics in your digital marketing strategy. Web analytics programs like Google Analytics can help you understand your customers' behavior, what they want, and how they interact with your store. This data can guide you on where improvements are needed and how to deliver a better customer experience.

Remember, a successful digital marketing strategy for your eCommerce store takes time and requires consistent effort. Be ready to consistently experiment, learn and optimize your efforts to reach your desired success.

Chapter 13. Scaling Up: Managing Your Growing eCommerce Store

A crucial phase of launching your own successful eCommerce store is scaling up. But managing a growing eCommerce store is not an easy task. It involves a wide array of tasks such as inventory management, customer service enhancement, employing automation, optimizing for SEO, and so on.

13.1. Set Clear Growth Goals

When you start scaling your eCommerce store, your first task should be setting clear growth goals. If you don't know where you're heading, it can make your path towards growth confusing and uncertain. Make sure you have clear short-term and long-term goals that align with your overall business strategy.

You might choose your goals based on revenue, sales units, site visitors, or even social media followers — these all depend on what's most important to your specific business model. Once you've defined your goals, ensure they're measurable, as this will allow you to have a clear idea of your progress.

13.2. Develop a Scalable Business Model

Without a scalable business model, your business could have difficulty growing, or you may find that growth is not as profitable as you hoped. A scalable business model should be designed in such a way that your operating costs don't increase significantly as your business grows, leading to increased profitability as sales increase.

A scalable business model should be flexible in accommodating growth, such as adding new products or entering new markets without disrupting current operations. It should also consider any potential partnerships or affiliations that could help boost your business growth and leverage these collaborations effectively.

13.3. Employ Automation

As your eCommerce store grows, manual efforts may not be enough to manage every task. From inventory management to customer service, automation can save time and increase efficiency.

Inventory management software can track product availability and help with reordering before stocks run out. Automation tools for customer service, like chatbots, can handle basic customer queries round the clock, freeing your team up for more complex customer issues.

13.4. SEO Optimisation

Making your site and products findable by search engines is one of the best ways to attract organic traffic. Several aspects of your site should be optimised for SEO: page titles, meta descriptions, URL structure, alt tags on images, and product descriptions.

Product descriptions should incorporate keywords and phrases that potential customers are likely to search for. However, avoid keyword stuffing which may decrease your site's SEO performance. Regular blogging related to your products or industry can also boost your SEO.

13.5. Optimize Site Performance

As your eCommerce store grows, you might find that your website starts to slow down, especially during periods of high traffic. A slow website can frustrate customers and increase cart abandonment rates - both detrimental to growth.

Consider migrating to a more robust web hosting service that can handle high traffic volumes. And ensure your site design is optimized for speed – large images and complicated designs can significantly slow down page load times.

13.6. Enhancing Customer Service

Customer service is paramount for keeping your clients loyal to your store. Make sure you have a dedicated and skilled team to handle all customer queries and complaints effectively. Live chat, FAQ sections, and easy-to-find contact information enhance the customer experience on your site.

13.7. Adapting Business Plan

As your business grows, your business plan should evolve. Your initial business plan might have served to establish your business, but as you scale up, you'd need to adapt it according to changing market conditions, customer behaviors, and industry trends.

Review your business plan regularly, keeping an eye on changing trends in your target demographic, fluctuations in market conditions, and new technologies or practices in eCommerce.

Scaling up your eCommerce store presents numerous challenges, but with clear goals and a flexible business model, smart use of automation, effective SEO, optimal site performance, excellent customer service, and a flexible business plan, you can manage your growing online store and be on your way to eCommerce success.

www.ingramcontent.com/pod-product-compliance
Lightning Source LLC
Chambersburg PA
CBHW071015260726
48661CB00007B/2983